# WEATHER FACT FRENZY!

by Jaclyn Jaycox

CAPSTONE PRESS
a capstone imprint

Published by Capstone Press, an imprint of Capstone
1710 Roe Crest Drive, North Mankato, Minnesota 56003
capstonepub.com

*Weather Fact Frenzy!* was originally published as *Totally Amazing Facts About Weather*, copyright 2018 by Capstone Press.



Library of Congress Cataloging-in-Publication Data is available on the Library of Congress website.

ISBN: 9798875254888 (hardcover)
ISBN: 9798875254833 (paperback)
ISBN: 9798875254840 (ebook PDF)

Summary: There's a WEATHER FACT FRENZY headed your way! Did you know that certain weather conditions can make it rain frogs? Or that there's a hurricane on Jupiter that's larger than Earth? Whether you're in the mood to browse or to devour a book from cover to cover, you're sure to learn some fascinating weather science as you blow through these pages!

Editorial Credits
Designer: Jaime Willems; Media Researcher: Svetlana Zhurkin; Production Specialist: Whitney Schaefer

Image Credits
Associated Press: Pat Wellenbach, 56; Getty Images: Architectural Visualization, 58, Bryan Godfrey, 41, Gregory_Dubus, 62, MathieuRivrin, 36, Miha9000, 60, Mike Hollingshead, 49 (middle), Mike Lyvers, 33, miniseries, 51, Stocktrek Images, 42 (top), Vincenzo De Palo Photo, 32; Shutterstock: Adansijav Official, 50 (map), ajt, 1 (top), All a Shutter, 21, alle, 13 (bottom), Andrei Stepanov, 9, Anterovium, 14, Aroonsak, 47, Arrow K Co, 15 (bottom), Arthit Premprayot, 11 (bottom), Artsiom P, 39, Atosan, 24 (top), Benny Marty, 28, Best-Backgrounds, 38, bodom, 22, BrAt82, cover (TV), Cammie Czuchnicki, 44, CkyBe (speech bubble), 5 and throughout, cobalt88, 13 (middle), daulon, 34, Dmitry Chulov, 23, eddtoro, 57, EnviroSense, 7, Eric Isselee, 53, Filip Bjorkman, 37 (top), float (weather icons), 5 (bottom) and throughout, FootMade0525, 4 (left), Gfx Expert Team (tornado), 3, 45, 50, gn8 (rays and lines), cover and throughout, Gorobets, 42 (bottom), Gorodenkoff, cover (weather map), GraphicsRF, 35, Guppic the duck, cover (bow, sunglasses), Helioscribe, 54, Idea Route, cover (top left), Igor Tarasyuk, 20, IgorZh, 29, Irfan0416, back cover, 4 (right), Irina Gutyryak, cover (bottom right), 4 (middle), 64, Japan's Fireworks, 24 (bottom), John D Sirlin, 18, Joseph Sohm, 43, Kichigin, 1 (bottom), 55 (top), Kolonko, 24 (middle), Lukas Jonaitis, 27, MarkoBabii (weather icons), cover, back cover, Matt Gush, 6, Maximillian cabinet, 16, Md. Sykhul Islam Shamim, 63 (clouds), Michal Ludwiczak, cover (middle right), Natalya Aksenova, 45 (chickens), Nerthuz, 19, Newtonian, 48, Nomad_Soul, 30, omkuhh, cover (middle left), photka, 10, Photoongraphy, 12, plampy, cover (lightning), posmguys, 63 (cannon), Que Images, 17, Rainer Lesniewski, 11 (middle), Rob Atherton, 52, Sarin Kunthong, 59, Sherry Saye, 25, Shirley Jayne Photography, 37 (middle), Silverszay, 46, Siwakorn1933, 45 (feathers), Steven Group, 8, Suzanne Tucker, 61, TrapezaStudio, 55 (bottom), Triff, 31, v_kulieva (gradient background), back cover and throughout, valdezrl, 26, Wirestock Creators, 15 (middle), Yuliya D'yakova, 5 (top), Zdenek Sasek, 49 (bottom), zstock, 40



Printed and bound in China. PO 6461

# TABLE OF CONTENTS

# A FLOOD OF INFORMATION ABOUT WEATHER!

"When it rains, it pours." "It's raining cats and dogs!" Many common expressions (and the names of LOTS of sports teams!) are inspired by what comes out of the sky. Weather is something people love, hate, and even hide from! So, how much do you know about the winds and water that swirl around our planet? Discover the answers to all kinds of weather mysteries—like which insect can tell you the temp, and what on Earth a haboob is!

PULL OUT YOUR UMBRELLA—YOU'RE ABOUT TO GET FLOODED WITH A FRENZY OF WEATHER FACTS!

# WHAT'S IN THE FORECAST?

Yuma, Arizona, is the sunniest place on Earth. It receives more than 4,000 hours of sunshine per year!

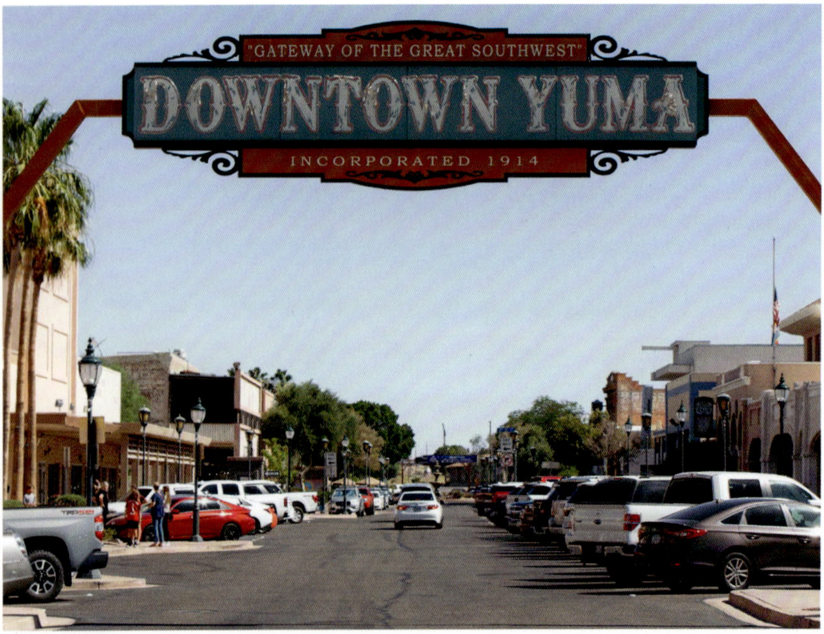

Commonwealth Bay, Antarctica, is the windiest place on Earth.

Winds of 200 miles (322 kilometers) per hour have been recorded there—the speed of an EF5 tornado!

The hottest temperature ever recorded was in Death Valley, California. On July 10, 1913, it reached 134° Fahrenheit (56.7° Celsius).

The coldest temperature recorded in a populated area reached -90°F (-68°C) in Siberia, Russia.

**WOW!**

Antarctica had a record-cold temperature of -128.6°F (-89.2°C) in July 1983. If you spit in this temp, your spit would freeze before hitting the ground!

Early TV weather forecasters used hand puppets to report the weather.

On average, seven-day weather forecasts are right about 80 percent of the time. (When a forecast is wrong, it's called a "bust.")

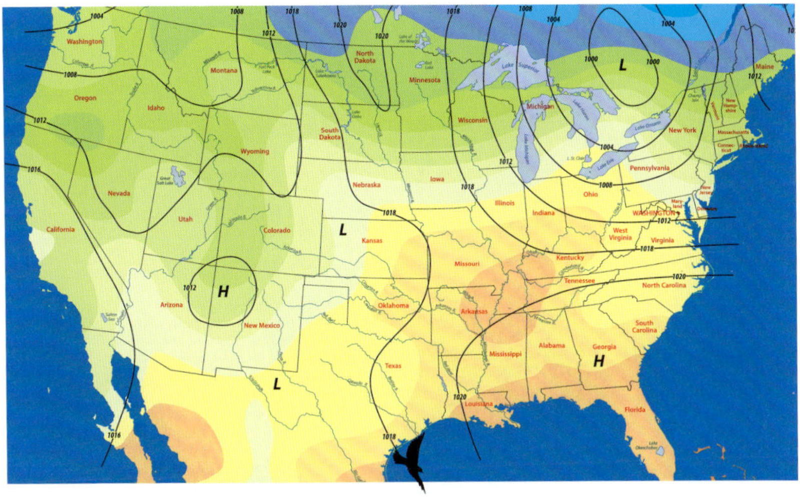


Weather radar has been known to pick up flocks of migrating birds and huge swarms of bugs!

Earth is in the "Goldilocks zone." Its distance from the sun makes it not too hot, too cold, too wet, or too dry—it's *just right* to host life-forms.

Oddly enough, the start of winter for the northern hemisphere is in December, when Earth is *closest* to the sun.

A cricket can tell you the temperature in Fahrenheit! Just count the number of chirps in 15 seconds, then add 40.

Aurora borealis (the northern lights) and aurora australis (the southern lights), are caused by collisions of particles in Earth's atmosphere.

A moonbow is a rare rainbow that appears at night, created by light from the moon.

Sun dogs look like a pair of very bright spots on either side of the sun. They're most often seen in cold weather when the sun is low in the sky.

A mix of wind and dirt can create dust storms called "black blizzards."

A black blizzard dropped 6,000 tons (5,443 metric tons) of soil on Chicago in 1934.

Dust devils are like little tornadoes, but these whirlwinds of air and sand are usually harmless.

Dust storms in the Sahara can blow a dust wall 1 mile (1.6 km) high!

A giant wall of blowing dust is called a "haboob."

Neptune has the strongest winds in the solar system. Its winds have been clocked at 1,200 miles (1,931 km) per hour!

# RAIN AND THUNDER

Raindrops are shaped like hamburger buns when they fall. They fall at about 20 miles (32 km) per hour.

Rain can carry desert sand, which turns the rain red. It looks like it's raining blood!

A mountain in Kauai, Hawaii, is one of the wettest spots on Earth. It rains there up to 350 days each year.

A town in Maryland holds the record for the most rain in one minute. In 1956, 1.23 inches (3.12 centimeters) of rain fell in just 60 seconds.

India holds the record for the most rain in one year—1,000 inches (25.4 m).

**WOW!**

Arica, Chile, once went 14 years without rain!

Is that a UFO? Nope, it's a lenticular cloud.

A good-sized thundercloud weighs as much as 10,000 747 jets!

Cirrocumulus clouds look like fish scales.

Altocumulus clouds look like little castles in the sky.

Mammatus clouds hang from the belly of a cloud like a cow's udder.

There are about 16 million thunderstorms on Earth each year.

Roughly 2,000 thunderstorms can be happening on Earth at any given moment.

Lightning strikes about 100 times per second on Earth.

About 1 out of every 10 lightning bolts hits the ocean rather than land.

**WOW!**

A single flash of lightning has enough power to run a 100-watt light bulb for three months!

A lightning bolt is five times hotter than the sun!

Lightning can strike up to 25 miles (40 km) away from a storm.

People who have been hit by lightning have been blown out of their socks and shoes!

A park ranger named Roy Sullivan was struck by lightning seven times. Twice it started his hair on fire!

The chance of someone being hit by lightning just once in their lifetime is 1 in 15,300.

The Empire State Building in New York City is struck by lightning about 25 times per year. It was once struck eight times in 24 minutes!

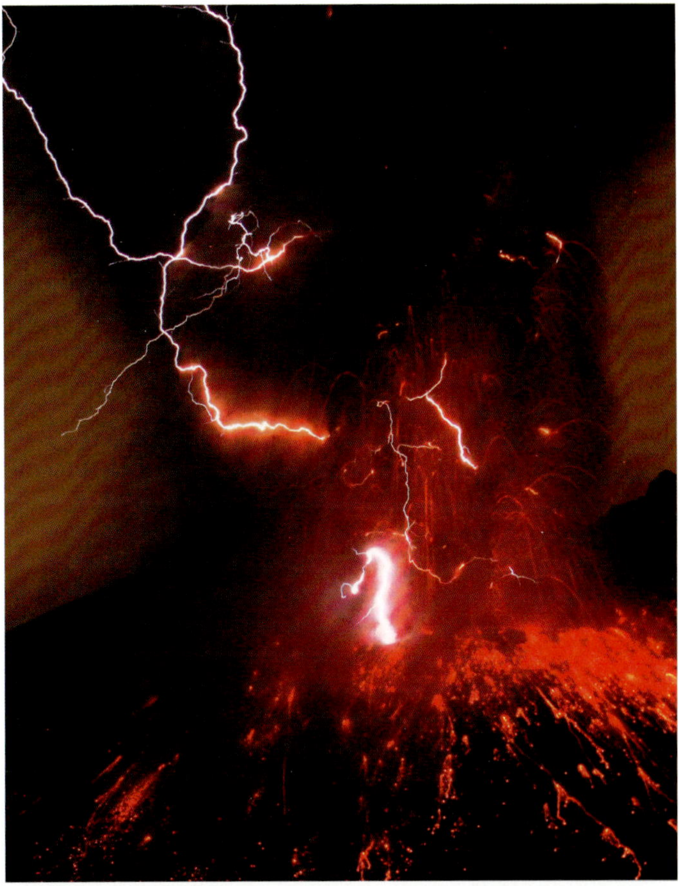

If there's lightning when a volcano erupts, it's called a "dirty thunderstorm."

# TSUNAMIS, HURRICANES, AND TORNADOES

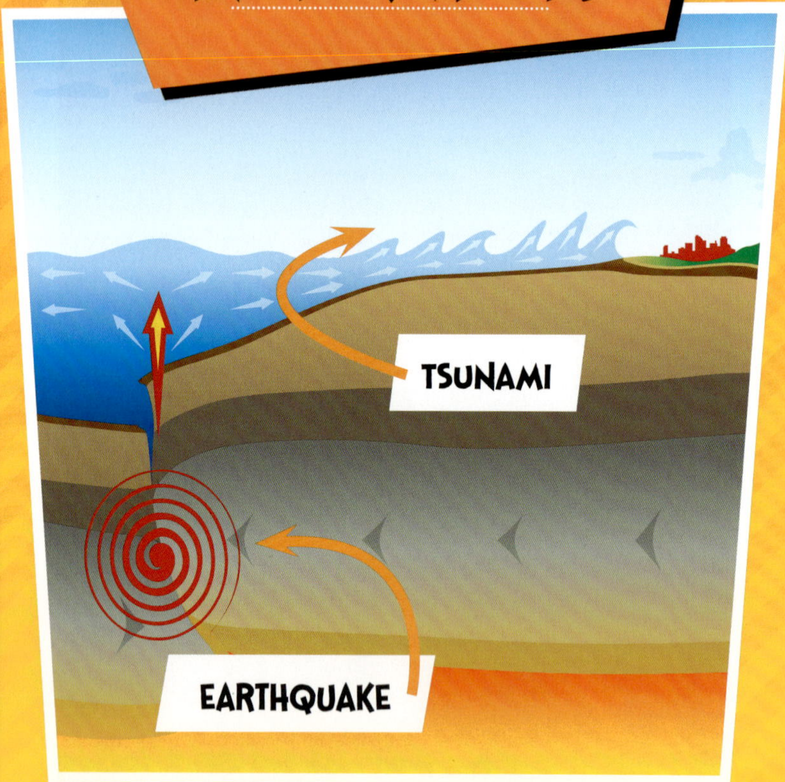


Tsunamis are created from an earthquake or volcanic eruption.

Waves from a tsunami can travel 450 miles (724 km) per hour!

In 2004 a huge earthquake caused a tsunami in the Indian Ocean. The deadliest in history, it killed more than 226,000 people and left millions homeless.

The word hurricane means "god of evil."

Typhoons are hurricanes that occur in the Northwest Pacific Ocean. Tropical cyclones are hurricanes in the South Pacific Ocean or Indian Ocean.

In Australia, hurricanes are called "willy-willies."

Hurricanes in the northern hemisphere rotate counterclockwise. In the southern hemisphere, they rotate clockwise.

The "eye" of a hurricane is usually calm. The area surrounding the eye is the most dangerous part.

A huge hurricane on Jupiter called the Great Red Spot is larger than Earth. It has been raging for more than 300 years!

The fastest wind speed recorded on Earth happened in 1996 during a tropical cyclone. It hit Australia with winds of 253 miles (407 km) per hour.

A storm surge during a hurricane can reach more than 20 feet (6 m) high.

WOW!

A large hurricane releases the energy of 10 atomic bombs every second!

The costliest hurricane in the world was Hurricane Katrina. The damage totaled more than $191 billion.

Hurricane Ivan caused a record 127 tornadoes to sprout over nine U.S. states. Nearly 90 percent of the deaths from hurricanes are a result of flooding, not wind.

A 1979 tropical cyclone called Typhoon Tip was the largest storm ever on Earth. It was almost half the size of the United States!

The Enhanced Fujita Scale measures the strength of tornadoes. The weakest tornado is an EF0. The strongest is an EF5.

EF5 tornadoes have wind gusts of more than 200 miles (322 km) per hour. The strongest tornadoes can toss cars around like toys.

Tornadoes have been known to pluck the feathers off of chickens!

Tornadoes form from thunderstorms called supercells. A tornado can last a few seconds to as long as three hours.

Like hurricanes, most tornadoes in the northern hemisphere rotate counterclockwise. In the southern hemisphere, they rotate clockwise.

A tornado's funnel can take different shapes. Sometimes a funnel looks like an elephant's trunk coming out of a cloud.

The widest tornado ever recorded was in Oklahoma in 2013. It was 2.6 miles (4.2 km) wide. That's wider than 45 U.S. football fields!

The deadliest tornado on record happened in Bangladesh in 1989. It killed 1,300 people.

Some people say tornadoes sound like a million bumblebees. Others say they sound like 1,000 jet engines.

Each year about 1,200 tornadoes occur in the United States. That's about 75 percent of the total twisters on Earth each year.

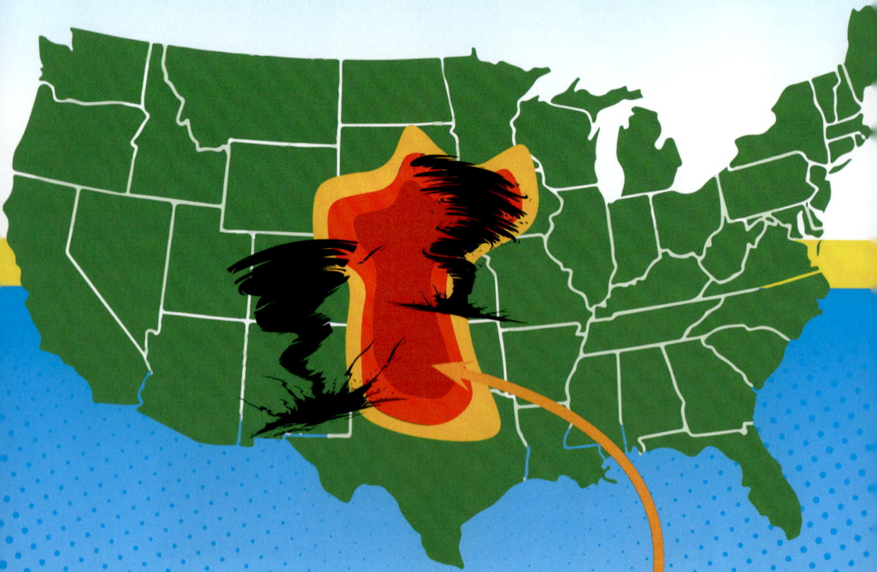

The U.S. Great Plains region has been called "Tornado Alley."

Some people believe that cats and dogs can sense when a tornado is coming.

Waterspouts are a type of tornado that happens over water.

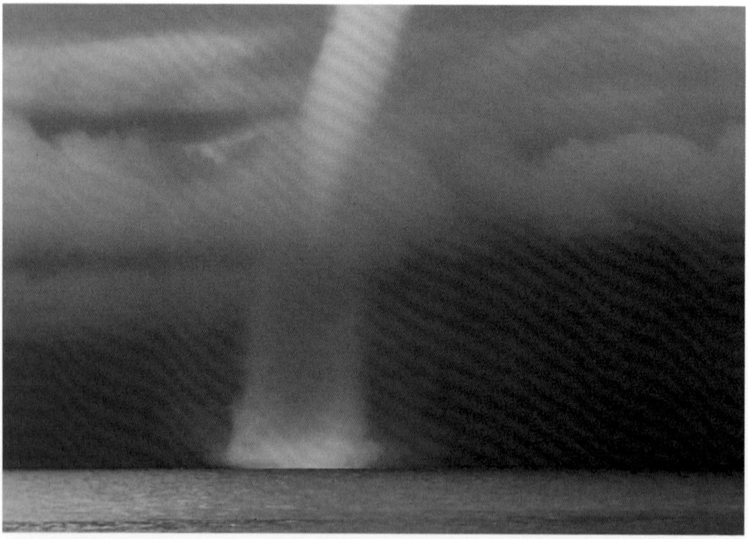

Florida is known as the waterspout capital of the United States. About 500 waterspouts occur there each year.

It once rained frogs in England because of a waterspout! In other parts of the world, it has also rained fish, worms, and even alligators!

# SNOW AND ICE

Just 1 inch (2.5 cm) of rain is equal to 13 inches (33 cm) of fluffy snow.

A falling snowflake can take one hour to reach the ground.

If it lands on water, a snowflake screeches. (But the sound is too high-pitched for humans to hear.)

According to the Guinness Book of World Records, the largest snowflake ever was 15 inches (38 cm) wide—about the size of a large pizza!

Olympia, the tallest snowwoman in the world was built in Maine. She weighed 13 million pounds (5.9 million kilograms) and was 122 feet (37 m) tall. (That's taller than the heel-to-head height of the Statue of Liberty!)

Winter storms along the U.S. east coast are known as "nor'easters." They can bring feet of snow and hurricane-like winds.

Syracuse, New York, is the snowiest city in the United States.

Aomori City, Japan, is the snowiest place on Earth. An average of 312 inches (792 cm) of snow is dumped on the city each year.

The deadliest blizzard happened in southern Iran in 1972. During that storm, 26 feet (7.9 m) of snow fell and 4,000 lives were lost. Two whole towns had no survivors.

Extreme ice storms can cause as much damage as a tornado.

During an ice storm, just a half-inch (1.3 cm) of ice can add 500 pounds (227 kg) of weight to power lines!

Hailstones zing around inside a thunderstorm like bouncy balls until they are heavy enough to fall.

The largest hailstones on record weighed 2 pounds, 4 ounces (1 kg). They fell in Bangladesh and killed 92 people.

WOW!

Kericho, Kenya, holds the record for the most hail. It once saw 132 days of hail in one year.

In the 1700s, people fired cannons into clouds to try to prevent hail. It didn't work.

# BOOKS IN THIS SERIES